HIS EYES ARE ON THE SPARROW

Inspirational Poems
By Faun Franklin

Copyright © 2010 by Faun Franklin

His Eyes Are On The Sparrow
Inspirational Poems
by Faun Franklin

Printed in the United States of America

ISBN 9781612151182

All rights reserved solely by the author. The author guarantees all contents are original and do not infringe upon the legal rights of any other person or work. No part of this book may be reproduced in any form without the permission of the author. The views expressed in this book are not necessarily those of the publisher.

Unless otherwise indicated, Bible quotations are taken from The King James Version. Copyright © 1968 by The World Publishing Company.

www.xulonpress.com

- Dedicated to Pauline Brooks.

She taught me that no matter what trials or tribulations come our way we are able to do all things in Christ who strengthens us.

INTRODUCTION

What a mighty God we have. A God who sees every sparrow that falls. A God that knows every hair on our head and has them numbered. A God, who in such a vast universe, knows every star and has named them accordingly. A God so mighty that one day he will raise every living soul that has breathed the breath of life. Today with all the miracles God has allowed us to see, many still doubt his existence and sovereignty. In a world filled with violence, war, hate, crime, poverty, famine, disease, and catastrophes one would think a greater awareness of God would be acknowledged. Yet, still in his mercy and grace he allows us to carry on. If we look through spiritual eyes, God will help us see his divine plan and lead us through the trials and tribulations we shall encounter.

For we are troubled on every side, yet not distressed, we are perplexed, but not in despair; persecuted, but not forsaken; cast down, but not destroyed.
II Corinthians 4: 8-9.

My prayer is that these inspirational poems will touch and bless your life in such a way that it will give you encouragement in times of despair. Many of these poems were written about true events that actually occurred.

REMEMBERING THOSE THAT HAVE PASSED…

For we know that if our earthly house of this tabernacle were dissolved, we have a building of God, an house not made with hands, eternal in the Heavens.
II Corinthians 5:1

Grandmother's Last Days

My grandmother, Leona Brooks, dedicated her life in service to others.

Her willingness to keep her faith was most apparent in her last days spent on earth. With her last breath of life she praised God and glorified him, a testimony to all who knew her. I myself was strengthened and moved by God's power in grandmother's life, her unselfish nature seemed to beam through even during the last moments of her life. Her last wishes were for Bible reading; favorite gospel songs to be sung and bedside prayer that God soon would take her home to be with him. The day grandmother died she saw the face of Jesus and sounds of distant thunder rolling, I believe the thunder she heard was Jesus calling her home.

Grandmother's Last Days

The cross that she carried never in strife,
Was given in services all of her life.
Her body was worn her face showed great pain,
Still she praised Jesus for eternal things gained.

Her head lost its strength and her body grew weak,
Still her sweet spirit stayed gentle and meek.
Just open the door and let me slip in,
I'll cross over the river away from this sin.

She lifted her hands and praised God for his love,

Then she asked him to take her to Jesus above.
"Lord in your arms hold me softly" she'd say,
"Oh why must you tarry?" I'm ready today.

Day after day she suffered great loss,
Yet still cherished Jesus and what he did on the cross.
A verse from the Bible, a hymn of a song,
A prayer by her bedside these helped her along.

The thunder did roll; grandmother heard it that day,
And yes Jesus came and she flew away.
My days will be lonely and some will seem long,

But to wish her back here would only be wrong.

For now up in Heaven she's awaiting for me,

Joined with loved ones soon I will see.

Grandmother's Last Gift

The day before my grandmother died I gave her a single rose; a rose my husband had given to me the day before. The rose reminded me that all things, no matter how beautiful must die. This special gift I gave to grandmother. I placed it in her room upon her dresser. I would catch her glancing up at the rose as if she somehow knew this would be her last gift. The next day grandmother died; the rose also faded and died. I kept the dried rose placing it in my china cabinet. Often, I look at the dried rose knowing that in God's rose garden the rose will never die and in his garden grandmother lives walking among the roses.

Grandmother's Last Gift

The rose I sent was my goodbye,
The day before grandmother died.
But at the time I did not know,
Her last gift would be my rose…

This single rose with ruby blooms,
Sent its fragrance through her room.
Velvet pedals a smell that lingered,
A work of art by God's own finger.

Its beauty tender gently feels,
Within our hearts a joy instills.
For this reason when we die,
Upon our caskets roses lie.

A lovely grace they so bestow,

No other greater than the rose,

For all of us that trust in faith,

Christ the Rose of Sharon waits.

With his own blood our sins he'll pardon,

So we may enter God's rose garden.

The Baby Grace

Upon receiving a call from a dear Christian friend, Julia Nettles, I was asked to pray for her sister's baby that was soon to be born. The parent's had been informed that the baby would be born with a severe chromosome disorder, in which the life of the baby would be shortened. The parents were devastated, but patiently, trusting in God, waited for the baby to arrive. Soon after, Juliana Grace was born, she lived only 3 ½ weeks. The death of Baby Grace made such an impact upon many lives. I never saw Baby Grace but her life short as it was touched my life in a powerful way. I heard that shortly after the death of Baby Grace, a woman that attended her funeral gave her life to Christ. How amazing our Lord is! He uses the physical death of one to bring spiritual life to another. The short life of Baby Grace was not in vain.

The Baby Grace

I never saw her precious face,

Yet loved the baby they called Grace.

The word Grace means unmerited favor,

This the name her parents gave her,

Her little body that was lame,

Blessed with such a perfect name.

This little vessel from above,

Taught so many greater love,

Her days were numbered, not in vain,

And now in Heaven Grace does reign.

God gives us life and takes it away,

For his the potter and we're the clay.

Though her life was short in season,

God sent her here for his own reason.

His Eyes Are On The Sparrow

Grace was molded for a plan,

Created by the Master's hand.

Little Grace loved and missed,

Her parents once again shall kiss,

Her body whole without a flaw,

Unlike the one that they once saw.

So many times a child is taken,

Parents left feeling forsaken,

And though they do not understand,

Their baby lives in Beulah land.

For it is God who calls them home,

So in his kingdom they can roam.

While down on earth the parents wait,

Trusting their lord with hope and faith.

Believing in the words God said,

That he will surely raise the dead.

It's in a fairer greater place,

God smiles upon the baby Grace.

Baby Brother Brent

My mother seldom talks about the death of her first born child, Brent.

Brent died in childbirth some 48 years ago, a beautiful 10 lb. baby boy taken for no apparent reason. Today, that event still bears heavy upon the heart of my mother. Mother recalls the strong sense of God's presence in her hospital room the day Brent died. She heard what she accounts as Heavenly music which played seemingly out of the walls of her hospital room. The music she described as angelic, music from Heaven's realm. No one else ever heard this music, only her. I'm confident that the music mother heard that day was from above. Through the years, this recollection has given my mother the assurance of God's love and presence in what was the most difficult time of her life the loss of her firstborn son.

Baby Brother Brent

Little Brent my baby brother,
Was taken from my dad and mother.
Delivered back to God above,
The babe my parents greatly loved.

He never got to walk the earth,
Their first born died in child birth.
This little one with hair of gold,
My mother never got to hold.

Inside the room where mother stayed,
She heard sweet music gently play,
Her broken heart touched by this sound,
She felt God's presence all around.

His Eyes Are On The Sparrow

They placed her little angel's head,
Inside a tiny coffin bed.
One made a bonnet trimmed in lace,
To rap around his angel face.

My parents took from off his grave,
Little flowers that they could save.
So often they would take a look,
These pedals in Brent's baby book.

I recall what one once said,
"Its good we cannot look ahead",
To times in life when tried and tested,
To things so often greatly vested.

For in all things we can be strong,
Through Christ who helps us carry on,
And with this hope we know one day
That death itself shall pass away.

ALL HAIL THE POWER OF JESUS NAME

There's no other name in earth or in heaven like unto the name of Jesus. God who came down out of the portals of heaven to earth for one purpose to take upon himself, perfect as he was, the sins of all mankind. No greater love ever known than the love that Jesus shown.

Then opened he their understanding, that they might understand the scriptures,
And said unto them, thus it is written, and thus it beloved Christ to suffer, and to rise from the dead the third day:
And that repentance and remission of sins should be preached in his name among all nations, beginning at Jerusalem.

And ye are witnesses of these things.

And, behold, I send the promise of my Father upon you: but tarry ye in the city of Jerusalem, until ye be endued with power from on high.
Luke 24:45-49

This same Jesus who came, died and arose is coming back again.

But ye shall receive power, after that the Holy Ghost is come upon you: and ye shall be witnesses unto me both in Jerusalem, and in all Judaea, and in Samaria, and unto the uttermost part of the earth.
And when he had spoken these things, while they beheld, he was taken up; and a cloud received him out of their sight.

And while they looked steadfastly toward heaven as he went up, behold, two men stood by them in white apparel; which also said, ye men of Galilee, why stand ye gazing up into heaven? This same Jesus, which is taken up from you into heaven, shall so come in like manner as ye have seen him go into heaven.

Acts 1:8-11

The Greatest Story Ever Told

It happened some 2,000 years ago,

And it's the greatest story that's ever been told.

He didn't have fame nor did he have wealth,

He had no desire to glorify self.

One purpose he had was to die on a tree,

That all could be saved who are like you and me.

His gospel was simple his message was clear,

If you come to me know you have nothing to fear.

Yet many rejected and called him bad names,

Even those who had seen him heal the sick and the lame.

The pain that he suffered driven nails in his hands,
Was part of his mission on earth as a man.

They ripped off his shroud,
And put thorns in his brow,
Our Lord took on shame when we were to blame.
Perfect he was even when he died,
Yet many today in sin still do hide.

Why can't we see what he tried to show?
And give more of our love that others will know.
But today scoffers mock him their numbers are great,
They make light of wisdom and try to take away faith,

They say where's his coming? The raptures a lie,
And that Jesus was never really crucified.

They call all the Christians stupid and dumb,
And they say that our Lord isn't going to come,
But what will they do when they come to Hell's gates?
And then there they realize it's all but to late,

For all of the damage has already been done,
And they'll scream out from Hell,
"He was really the Son!"

Only One

One who came down to this earth,
And angels hailed his holy birth,
One who showed that he did care,
One who sent his Son not spared,
One sent from God his Son so blessed,
A dove that gently on him rest.

One who made the waters still,
One who gave man free will,
One who calms the ocean waves,
And brought the dead out of their graves.

One who caused the blind to see,
One who came from Galilee,
One who fasted forty days,
Never tempted, never strayed.

His Eyes Are On The Sparrow

One who made the water wine,
One who touched and healed the blind,
One who shed his blood for man,
Parted the sea with his own hands.

One who did not fear to tell,
A woman that was at the well,
Water that would give her life,
Despite her sin that brought her strife.

One who walked upon the sea,
One who sets the captives free,
One who made the deaf to hear,
One who demons still do fear.

His Eyes Are On The Sparrow

One who put the stars in place,

And loves us with unchanging grace,

One who takes away our pride,

One who all our sins will hide.

One who died upon a tree,

Upon the hill of Calvary,

One who now in Heaven waits,

Inside the city's Pearly Gates.

One the Father soon will send,

One whose coming back again,

One whose part and in three,

Blessed is the Trinity.

The Father's Dear Son

No one should be lifted, honored or praised,
Except it be Jesus God resurrected and raised.
God's has no respect of person we easily fall,
Yet still man through Jesus God so diligently calls.

The called ones they labor for the souls that's unsaved,
Praying by faith they'll accept what God gave.
Humbled and gentle, gracious and meek,
These are the fruits of the children God seeks.

Knowing we must be born from above,
Through the cross Jesus carried in agape type love,

Sealed up in faith by God's Son who is King,
Protected by hosts of angelic wings.

God's only begotten Son he did give,
Through his precious blood we eternally live.
No greater love has ever been known,
Than the love of the Father so graciously shown.

So help us dear Savior to love one another,
And through a kind spirit except all our brother,
For we can't be your witness if were filled up with hate,
Against other humans the Lord did so create.
In God's heavenly kingdom we'll all be as one,
But only through Jesus the Father's dear Son.

Beyond The Heaven's Doors

I walked outside to get the mail,
The ground it shook and then I fell,
Things they happened oh so fast,
I saw a glimpse of all my past.

My head was spinning like a wheel,
My body felt a strange ordeal,
Without a word, without a pause,
I felt as if I had no cause.

My eyes were taken by the light,
And then I saw a glorious sight,
As Christ appeared arrayed in white,
In beams of glory shown so bright.

His Eyes Are On The Sparrow

The graves they opened everywhere,

With bodies immortal Christ-like bared,

They shot like arrows in the air,

A number far beyond compare,

To meet their souls forever more,

And go beyond the Heaven's doors.

Oh like an eagle to the sky,

I seemed to take on wings to fly,

I felt my flesh in mid-air change,

All myself was re-arranged.

All the beauty I once read,

Now floated all around my head,

For we were taken through a hole,

And at its end it looked like gold,

More than I could ever dream,

Was those I loved and now I see,

His Eyes Are On The Sparrow

Earthly past could never be,
Like Heaven's radiant eternity.

To think of minutes only past,
This feeling ever more shall last,
But what of those who did not see,
That Christ he died for you and me.

If we had shared the blessed news,
Maybe then there'd be but few,
If now on earth before these days,
Will leave for Christ and teach his ways,
Then maybe more will then be saved,
And go the road that Jesus paved.

So let the light of Christ shine through,
That some will see the Lord in you,
And I will meet you some sweet day,
In God's great mansions far away.

Feed My Sheep

Quickly children move your feet,
Take my word and feed my sheep,
Take the message, open, show,
To a world that does not know.
Take my word to other lands,
Gently place it in their hands.

While some may sew and some may reap,
God will help us feed his sheep.
Lord let us all be aware,
Of the devil's evil snare,
For in our lives he'll try to creep,
So we won't go and feed your sheep.

Oh help us Lord to not be weak,

The enemy we can defeat if your word is rooted deep,

Help us lord to feed the sheep.

What great joy the angels feel,

When to them God does reveal,

And to the saints that watch and weep,

When God brings home but one lost sheep.

Let us often to God pray,

For the sheep gone astray,

That his sheep will soon be found,

Then in Gods Kingdom there abound,

Protected by the Shepherds touch,

By his hands that love so much,

Lets shout in Heaven when we meet,

Great be the number of the sheep.

A Glimpse of Heaven

It wasn't all inside my head,
They really did pronounce me dead.
I stood beside the throne of God,
And walked where angels often trod.

The choir was loud and they did sing,
Praises to the Lord and King,
I felt my spirit light and free,
Could this be eternal me?

A greater peace was in my mind,
That down on earth I'd tried to find,
The beauty that surrounded me,
My earthly eyes did never see.

His Eyes Are On The Sparrow

I saw my aunt, my great grandmother,
And then I saw my baby brother.
Then something deep inside of me,
Made me never want to leave.

I thought of what I had on earth,
My possessions and there worth,
I'd give it all to stay right here,
To never have another fear.

Then a voice said to me,
"It's not your time you need to leave",
But some fair day you'll come again,
And then the victory you will win.
Like a flash I was gone,
Back to the life where I belonged,
All these things that I had seen,
Were not just a crazy dream.

WHY DO GOD'S CHILDREN SUFFER?

There is no set answer to the problem of why God's children suffer. God did not promise we would miss the storms of life, only that in the end we would win the victory if our foundation is built upon faith found in Jesus Christ the Lord. Scriptures state very clear, not only the fact that God's own suffer, but why his children suffer.

Many are the afflictions of the righteous, but the Lord delivereth him out of them all.
Psalms 34:19

These things I have spoken unto you, that in me ye might have peace. In the world ye shall have tribulation: but be of good cheer; I have overcome the world.
John 16:33

Yea, and all that will live godly in Christ Jesus shall suffer persecution.
II Timothy 3:12

Yea man is born unto trouble, as the sparks fly upward.
Job 5:7

But he knoweth the way that I take; when he hath tested me, I shall come forth as gold.
Job 23:10

For whom the Lord loveth he chasteneth, and scourgeth every son whom he receiveth. If ye endure chastening, God dealeth with you as with sons; for what son is he whom the father chasteneth not?
Hebrews 12:6-7

Furthermore, we have had fathers of our flesh who corrected us, and we gave them reverence. Shall we not much rather be in subjection unto the Father of Spirits, and live? For they verily for a few days chastened us after their own pleasure, but he for our profit, that we might be partakers of his holiness.
Now no chastening for the present seemeth to be joyous, but grievous; nevertheless, afterward it yieldeth the peaceable fruit of

righteousness unto them who are exercised thereby.
Hebrews 12:9-11

...But we glory in tribulations also, knowing that tribulation worketh patience.
Romans 5:3

The scriptures listed should help us to realize our Heavenly Father disciplines us for our own benefit. Through God's discipline we gain patience, assurance, spiritual profit and productivity which help us to be more faithful and productive Christians.

For we are to run with patience the race that is set before us. Looking unto Jesus, the author and finisher of our faith, who for the

joy that was set before him endured the cross, despising the shame, and is set down at the right hand of the throne of God.
Hebrews 12:2

Christ suffered more than any man could every have suffered, so that through him all can obtain eternal life.

The Great Physicians Touch

The day she came into this world,
I loved my precious baby girl.
Because the doctor was not there,
Her little arm they could not spare,
The nerves were severed, ripped, and torn,
The very day that she was born.

They took some x-rays on that day
And said her arm would stay that way,
This little arm would never mend,
Never to be used again.

With all of this we could not cope,
We turned to Jesus for our hope,
We saw God's people really cared,
With churches praying everywhere.

His Eyes Are On The Sparrow

We knew our lord without delay,
Would work it out in his own way,
By our bedside we did kneel,
And prayed God's power our child he'd heal.
We knew her arm was very weak,
But it was God, who we would seek.

Then on a very special day,
On the couch our baby laid,
Her little arm she lifted high,
All of us began to cry!

The doctors could not understand,
The Great Physician's mighty hand.
He has the power to touch and heal,
If we but ask it be his will.

I've never asked the question why?

Though many years have passed on by,

Reminded of what God did mend,

Within her arm a little bend.

I praise his mighty holy name,

He did not leave my Fallon lame.

The Rich Poor Beggar

I set along on crowded streets,

Watching all the busy feet,

Money dropped down by my side.

In the corner where I hide,

All I own is in a pack,

Strapped and carried on my back.

The people stop they look and pause,

At the man that has no cause.

My layered clothes are worn and old,

But they protect me from the cold.

I lack on earth material things,

But in my heart a voice does sing,

The day will come my soul will soar,

Beyond this earth to Heaven's door.

My treasures lie not here on earth,

In all life's money and its worth,

Christ's riches come from deep within,

Its earthly pleasures Satan sends,

Though now I'm such a wretched sight,

I'll then be clothed in garments white.

Only God can see the soul,

And if through Christ it's been made whole,

God will knock on all men's door,

Whether they be rich or poor.

Little Boy Blue the Whipping Child

Little Boy Blue his whipped and torn,
Never got to blow his horn.
Taken in by foster care,
To a life that's so unfair.

Little Boy Blue the whipping child,
Given drugs because you're wild,
Often in a corner stays,
Prays the day will pass away.

Little Boy Blue lives in a cage,
Beat by hands in acts of rage,
Little Boy Blue does often morn,
Wishes he was never born.
Little Boy Blue who bears this cup,
The day will come when you'll grow up.

His Eyes Are On The Sparrow

Little Boy Blue your worlds insane,

Tell sweet Jesus of your pain,

For he will never leave your side,

The little boy he'll gently guide,

Little Boy Blue oh don't you cry,

For Jesus all your tears will dry.

Fat Lady Sings

Could it be that it's too late?
Will I never lose this weight?
Oh dear Lord, please set me free,
The person that's inside of me.

I hear the people laughing loud,
When I am walking in a crowd.
They mock, they joke, they point and stare,
I act as though I'm not aware.

The Lord don't mind to him I'll cling,
This fat lady that longs to sing,
The fat that's clinging to my waist,
In his arms God will embrace,
Has this fat so sealed my fate?
In a world so full of hate,

I know in Heaven large or small,
That it won't matter then at all.

Life To Save

The war on hunger we should fight,
Before we take another bite.
The hour now is growing late,
We must put food upon more plates!

We must be willing to do more,
To help so many who are poor.
Taking food to help and fill,
These little souls that famine kills.

Great is the number, we can't count,
Yet still each day the number mounts,
For everyday a mother morns,
For the child that she has born.

His Eyes Are On The Sparrow

Should we be willing? Should we be able?

For we throw food from off our tables,

It's giving life to these in need,

These little mouths that we can feed.

Please don't let us hesitate,

While many hungry children wait,

For if we help the least of these,

It's the father, whom we please,

How great the blessing to be gained,

To those who help stop hungers pain.

Karla Tucker Brown

On Death row she waits her turn,

But it was here that Karla learned,

Living in a prison cell,

Without parole, without bail,

The demons in her life so dark,

Upon her life they made their mark,

To a fate upon death row.

From the crime in life she sewed,

Behind iron bars she came to see,

Of a love beyond degree,

That sets the vilest sinner free.

And know upon God's word she stands,

To be a voice in our land.

It does not matter what we've done,

God will forgive through Christ the Son.

Though death is knocking at her door,

She does not fear it anymore,

For death may be the final cost,

But her desires to touch the lost,

To show the world that God can touch,

The sinner who has done so much,

If they'll take their sin and plea,

The "Great I Am" will set them free,

The blood of one, who paid the cost,

Of the sinner that is lost.

Through The Valley

I felt the hand of Jesus touch me in my bed,
While thumbing through the scriptures of his word I often read.
I heard his voice so very clear,
I'll lift your doubt and take your fear,
For in this hour while sick and weak,
It is me you'll come to seek.

I am the Lord I do not wrong,
For in this trial I'll make you strong.
So please don't question what I do,
I know my child what is best for you.

I'll mold and shape your vessel right,
To glorify it in my sight,
I'll never ever leave your side,

His Eyes Are On The Sparrow

I'll be your constant steady guide,
I'll lift you high by my right hand,
And help you better understand.

If you think I do not care,
Remember child I hear all prayers,
And though the devil seems to lurk,
Right this hour I am at work.

Just trust me as your Savior consider me your friend,
For soon your health I shall restore your body I will mend,
The clouds so dark shall blow away,
And you will see a better day,
Though the valley might seem long,
It's through the valley God makes us strong.

It's Never Too Late

The little old man he sat alone,
Inside a room he called his home.
Outside the window cars flew by,
That made him ask the question why?

Then vivid thoughts of yesterday,
Inside his mind seemed to rage,
A body worn, a mind half gone,
He wondered what he'd done so wrong?

He thought of days back years ago,
But now he's left so aged and old.
He thought of things he might have changed,
If he could now but re-arrange.

His Eyes Are On The Sparrow

His bitter ways and jealous heart,
That made dear loved ones to impart.
A great desire for fame and wealth,
He didn't know they'd take his health.

Did all the money through the years,
Bring him joy or bring him tears?
His family that he left alone,
They now have lives of their own.

His wife that died so long ago,
Because of pain that he bestowed,
From a broken heart of grief,
That cut her life short and brief.

He never entered God's church doors,
Nor gave he money to the poor,
Nor did he care for no one else,

His Eyes Are On The Sparrow

He only cared for himself.

No one else could quite compare,

To this man who loved to swear.

Defiling words he use to say,

He wished he now could take away.

He never bragged or even boasts,

About the ones who loved him most.

All his life he wasted by,

He wished that God would let him die.

But then a voice small and still,

Whispered gently, "I love you Bill",

He looked around and saw no one,

And felt so bad for all he done,

He then remembered back when young,

About a God who sent his Son,

And how his mother use to pray,
That little Bill would soon be saved.

Then looking up to God above,
Bill realized Jesus' perfect love,
And with his mouth confession made,
All Bill's sins were washed away.

The Untouched Bible

The boy knew it was no fable,
That black book upon the table,
Handed down from years ago,
Its cover worn and very old.

The untouched Bible laying there,
Beside his grandma's rocking chair,
Never opened, never read,
No one knew what it said,
No one ever took a look,
At that little Holy Book.

No one really seemed to care,
That God's Word was even there,
Dust collected on its cover,
Never wiped away by mother,

But hide in pages it did hold,
All the things God so told.

Even though the book was closed,
The boy somehow seemed to know,
Inside these pages would unfold,
Everything that life does hold.

Never letting God's word in,
The boy grew up lost in sin,
Living life day by day,
Never bowing down to pray.

Then on his job one summer day,
A man explained the narrow way,
He showed the message so long hid,
From the man, once a kid,

With child like faith he believed,
Never more to be deceived.

Knowing now that he would gain,
From God's Word he took in vain,
Reading now every day,
The Holy scriptures God so gave,
And never more will he impart,
For now it's written in his heart.

POEMS OF PROPHESIES

In this century like no other, we have seen prophetic prophesies being fulfilled. End time events coming to pass like never before. The study of eschatology (end time events) is on the rise. God warns of great deception that will emerge toward the end of the age, I believe where seeing this deception as man's moral condition continues to falter. Today everyone is seeking for an answer, looking for a solution, trying to find a way to solve the existing problems of famine, violence and moral corruption plaguing our earth. Our principle standards today are being tested; we must be spiritually strong enough, in Christ, to pass the test. We are heading towards a climatic period God spoke of millennium's ago, a period in which Christ himself shall come and restore that which sin has destroyed. Man in his attempt to save himself shall fall and then realize when it's much too late that Christ really is the only answer.

This know also, that in the last days perilous times shall come.

For men shall be lovers of their own selves, covetous, boasters, proud, blasphemers, disobedient to parents, unthankful, unholy, without natural affection, truce breakers, false accusers, incontinent, fierce, despisers of those that are good,

Traitors, heady, high minded, lovers of pleasures more than lovers of God. Having a form of godliness, but denying the power thereof; from such turn away.

II Timothy 3: 1-5

For the time will come when they will not endure sound doctrine; but after their own lusts shall they heap to themselves teachers, having itching ears;

And they shall turn away their ears from the truth, and shall be turned unto fables.
II Timothy 4: 3-4

But there were false prophets also among the people, even as there shall be false teachers among you, who privily shall bring in damnable heresies, even denying the Lord that bought them, and bring upon themselves swift destruction.

And many shall follow their pernicious ways; by reason of whom the way of truth shall be evil spoken of.
II Peter 2: 1-2

That ye may be mindful of the words which were spoken before by the holy prophets and of the commandment of us the apostles of the Lord and Saviour:

Knowing this first, that there shall come in the last days scoffers, walking after their own lusts,

And saying, Where is the promise of his coming? For since the fathers fell asleep all things continue as they were from the beginning of the creation. For this they willingly are ignorant of, that by the word of God the heavens were of old, and the earth standing out of the water and in the water:

Whereby the world that then was, being overflowed with water, perished:

But the heavens and the earth, which are now, by the same word are kept in store, reserved

unto fire against the day of judgment and perdition of ungodly men.
II Peter 3: 2-7

Drawing Near

Today there's many filled with fear,
For end day signs are drawing near.
The earth is overcome with hate,
And many feel it's all too late.
The prophesies so long foretold,
Now on the earth seem to unfold.

We see the world so full of sin,
And know that soon God's Son he'll send,
The morning rooster starts to crow,
As man is running to and fro.
Knowledge seems to so increase,
An evil fury to unleash,
Upon the planet we call earth,
As now she goes in child birth.

The stars God set up in the sky,
Created by the one on high,
With power from Heaven he will shake,
While down on earth he'll send great quakes,
The sun and moon won't give their light,
Mid-day noon will seem like night.
Hurricanes gale force winds a devastation they will send,
Tornadoes forming in the air hitting places everywhere.
Heavy pouring unleashed rains,
Flooding over fields and plains.

For what will money then be worth,
When great destruction hits this earth?
For then a voice with power and might,
Will cause the world to then unite,

The earth will then become as one,
Casting out God the Son.

The Antichrist shall device and make,
A number man will have to take,
To trade, or sell, or even buy,
Without this number you will die.
It does not matter what some may say,
Let us learn to count our days,
And pray that worthy we shall be,
So Tribulation we want see.

Last Days

The days we are living are nearing there end,
And Christ when he left here said "I'm coming again".
The Lord will put evil under his feet,
Whatever you've sown is just what you'll reap.

Today news is scary, murder, violence and wars,
And catastrophes seem to be right at our doors.
What will it take for our world to awake?
Surely not another horrendous earthquake.

I can't help but think that people are blind,
And when it's too late then they'll see all the signs.

For while they are laughing and mocking with pride,
The saved will be entering in on the other side.
The lost will be left when the rapture soon comes,
And here they'll await the darkening sun,
For evil will reign when the saved are redeemed,
And those who are left here will be fooled and deceived.

The nations will fall under one possessed man,
He will use numbers on their foreheads and hands.
Then a great army the saints we shall be,
Christ will destroy him, and set captives free.

If all of us Christians would pray every day,

That loved ones and lost ones would come to be saved,

Then at the end of our numbered days,

Few would be left here lost and unsaved.

One Route

False religions setting in,
Cannot save a world from sin.
Sweeping like a powerful flood,
They can't redeem like Jesus blood.

These that's fallen by the way,
Will not believe that Jesus saves,
Giving up what they could know,
Taken in by Satan's foe.

They'll enter in the gate that's wide,
With neon lights on every side,
Rushing in without delay,
Not to the cross where sin was paid.

His Eyes Are On The Sparrow

Many having itching ears,

The truth they do not want to hear,

They listen to deceptive lies,

They'll cause the righteous ones to die,

Listen close and you will hear,

Approaching horsemen drawing near,

Knowing this is in God's will,

For latter things to be fulfilled.

Oh do not take the pagan's route,

But know without a single doubt,

That God his Son in love did give,

That life eternal we can live,

For greater is no other fame,

Wholly lean on Jesus' name.

The Living Water

I looked beyond the river it was flowing free,
The river I had long so known myself, my family,
The river it was clear, the bottom I could see,
Flowers bloomed around it to set its scenery.

The river flowed through meadows green and reached to other sands,
It gave clear fresh water to parched deserted lands,
Then one day some stones were dropped, soon there was a dam.
Then the river that once flowed free no longer fed the land,

The flowers by the river they withered up and died,

The meadows green in beauty lay desolate and dry.

All the land for miles around once painted by God's hand,

No longer had the fountains beneath the golden sands.

The water we drink freely in America today,

The communist are trying so hard to take away.

A stone dropped here, a stone dropped there and soon at our own door,

Would take away our beauty and make us weak and poor.

They'd take away the Word of God, the right of public prayer,

Then they'd teach our children not to love and not to care.

Like the other countries who didn't make a fist,
America the beautiful would fall to not exist.
Jesus Christ our Savior has blessed us with his grace,
And his water it runs freely to every single race.

The Little Church Upon the Hill

The little church upon the hill it's bell it rings no more,
The little church upon the hill they've bolted up its doors,
The little church upon the hill God's people filled its rooms,
Now only seems it was a dream its presence now so doomed.

The choir once it sang here old melodies in song,
But outside voices protested saying God's true Word was wrong.
The little church upon the hill does no one seem to care?

Does no one want to go there for God's sweet word to share?

The world is now to busy, it hasn't got the time,
For the little church upon the hill it will not spare a dime.
A little woman old and feeble goes to the church each week,
For she still longs the things of God and his good will to seek,
She kneels down by the alter and wonders what went wrong,
For no one ever comes here to lift their voice in song.

Her heart it grows so heavy and she thinks back to the past,

On how the people came here and why it didn't last.

She bows her head and says a prayer to the Father up above,

That he will bless this little church he gave to those he loved.

"We have a lot in common Lord this little church and me",

"For no one seems to care for us only Jesus, whom we seek",

She ends the prayer with these few words "Lord send back but a few",

Then brushes off the thickened dust gathered on the pew.

Apostasy has set in and I'm afraid my friends it's here,

So let us not be weary for its God that we should fear.

Let us pray to God above that he in his good will,

Shall watch, protect and greatly bless the church upon the hill.

Hale Bopp

Hale Bopp Comet passing by,
We can see up in the sky.
Just a star that's passing through,
A star Gods put within our view.

A cult under Satan's spell,
Believed a ship was at its tail,
Believed that an alien race,
Would take them to a better place.

How could these people be deceived?
The world could hardly but believe,
And some do think the end is near,
Because this comet has appeared.

His Eyes Are On The Sparrow

Oh the web that Satan spins,

Its man's soul he longs to win,

Devising up his evil lies,

And causing 30 more to die.

It's our lives he wants to take,

Our lives that God did so create.

Please in a star don't put your faith,

For 39 it's now too late.

GOD CREATOR OF CREATION

God's goodness is bestowed to us in his creation.

Life itself giving breath to everything great and small.

The herb and tree yielding seed,

The lights in the heavens, for signs, and for seasons, and for days, and years,

The fowl of the air,

The fish of the sea,

The beast of the earth and everything that creeps upon the earth.

In his own image God created man, a living soul.

In God's creation he was pleased.

God saw that it was good and blessed all things he created.

We're not to worship creation but the creator God who gave us the pleasures of creation we enjoy today.

What blessings we encounter everyday as we look around us enjoying these things God has created and has allowed us to be partakers of his beautiful world.

All things were made by him; and without him was not anything made that was made. In him was life; and the life was the light of men.
John 1:3-4

Heavens Music

I woke up just this morning to a very joyous sound,
The noise of something singing and fluttering around.
It made my heart so merry, it gave me quit a lift,
For the little bird was given as a special Christmas gift.

Singing birds are music given from God above,
A little part of Heaven for all of us to love.
God created them for springtime and for bright and sunny days,
Giving us much laughter in their small peculiar ways.

The Lord he sees each sparrow that falls down to the ground,

A part of Heaven loosing a great angelic sound.

The Master's Boutique

Springtime launches in the air,
Tiny seeds most everywhere,
These tiny seeds blow in to stay,
And in the meadows gently lay.

The seeds become little pods,
Touched by the hands of God,
Down in the valleys very low,
Gorgeous flowers start to grow.

God gives sunlight to touch their face,
Bringing beauties tender grace.
All these things they so employ,
The butterflies and bees enjoy.

His Eyes Are On The Sparrow

Picture paintings in our sight,

In green fields of color bright,

These boutique waves in pasture fields,

In our minds are locked and sealed.

For when the springtime ends its days,

These tender flowers fade away,

Yet knowing that another day,

They'll once again grace our way.

Winters Magic Powder

Winter's cold does greatly bear,
White flake flurries in the air.
Where the winds decide to blow,
Lands them on objects down below,
They lace the world in sheets of white,
Taking color out of sight.

The world once more will come aglow,
From nature's magic powder snow.
The children young and old at play,
In hopes the snow won't melt away.
Will lay in snow make angel wings,
While in a distance sleigh bells ring.

They'll ask the clouds to hide the sun,
While they make snowmen, Oh what fun!

Then bundle up so they want freeze,

From Mr. Winter's chilling breeze.

They'll pour hot chocolate in a cup,

Then very gently take a sup.

Their hands around the cup they'll hold,

To warm them from the bitter cold.

When temps go up the snow melts fast,

Like all good things it does not last.

Still out my window I will peer,

And pray for snow least once a year.

God's Golden Gift a Godly Other

Our lives are never perfect much sorrow comes our way,
But God has given mothers to take our fears away.
No one's life is perfect, but the love of mothers is,
Because only Godly mothers have the gift of care to give.

They hold you while you're little and never leave your side,
They take on all your burdens and never tell you lies.
They will kneel beside your bedside and pray to God above,

That he will guide, direct the path of the little ones they love.
They sing sweet songs of Jesus and lead us to the cross,
And hold our hands in sorrow when loved ones we have lost.

They teach us special scriptures, show us how to pray,
And lead us down a moral track so we will never stray.
They guide us through our school years, even when we're teens,
Protect us from the outside world that often can be mean.
They strive to give the best to us the things they never had,

And help us through the hard times that often seem so bad.

And when mother's hair turns silver and we look into her face,
We'll see the love God gave her and her sweet unchanging grace.
It's then we'll see so vividly the acts that she's so shown,
And all the fruits of labor that our mother often sewed.
Oh let us think, if we could be, the image of these saints,
The world would be a better place with far far less complaints.

My Child from Yesterday

The little girl of yesterday that use to come and want to play,
Who loved to sing inside the car and didn't want me off too far.
She use to crawl up in my bed,
She wanted special scriptures read,
Often times she'd say to me,
Mommy I will never leave.

The little cards her hands created are tucked away and most are dated,
With little hand prints stamped in paint from my little angel saint.
Remembering toys scattered everywhere,
Most of them where teddy bears.

His Eyes Are On The Sparrow

Frightful dreams filled with doom,

Sent her running to my room,

Up my bed she'd quickly crawl,

Pushing me into the wall,

The fear that took her by surprise,

Would make her under covers hide.

But soon the fear would go away,

Then still and quite she would lay.

She gave me wisdom from the start,

From little words that touched my heart.

She opened up a part of me

That gave me life and helped me see.

For just a moment she was small,

But now she's grown and oh how tall,

She doesn't ask for much advice,

There times she doesn't treat me nice,

Sometimes I look into her face,

And still the child wants to embrace,

This wise young lady she lives today,

She's still my child from yesterday.

Blessed To Be His Wife

I've never known a better man,
You always seem to understand.
The love you show shines through your ways,
Though you don't have a lot to say.

You work so hard provide a living,
A man of God so kind and giving.
Your hands in labor giving much,
Protected by God's mighty touch.

You're always there to lend a hand,
A gentle, willing, simple man.
On this earth I've never known,
A greater love than you have shown.

His Eyes Are On The Sparrow

Please understand I am aware,

Of all the burdens you so bare.

You've made my world a better place,

So all life's problems I can face,

For life's like sailing in a boat,

We must learn to stay afloat.

If we want to win life's battle,

The Lord must be the one to paddle.

I'm thankful Lord you heard my plea,

And brought this man of God to me.

I'm so blessed to be his wife,

Traveling through the sea of life.

The Simple Joys of Yesterday

The prize inside the box was hid,

From the girl the Cracker Jack Kid.

I loved the little sailor guy,

That wears around his neck a tie.

The golden box my favorite treat,

With nutty caramel popcorn sweet.

These treats I bought so many times,

Back then they cost but just one dime.

I remember way back when,

I wish today could be like then,

When children use to run and play,

The world today is not that way,

One didn't have to spend on toys,

The simple things could bring such joys.

His Eyes Are On The Sparrow

Our kids today find life a bore,

For they are rotten to the core.

The world today must be amused,

Its righteous morals we've abused.

The pace we live is much to fast,

Not like it was back in the past.

Imagine what the future holds,

If we refuse to change our goals,

I hate to think what is in store,

Or what is behind tomorrow's door.

If we don't change our evil ways,

A greater price we'll have to pay,

So let us turn back to the past,

For pleasures in this world don't last.

Life's Open Doors

Our lives are full of many doors we enter not in fear,
For God will let us know ahead before these doors draw near.

The open doors in front of us, they wait but just ahead,
We cannot see beyond these doors or where we might be led.

We know if we walk through these doors great things will be in store,
For God has paved the way for us to far and distant shores.

So many fear what they can't see they will not live in faith,
They'd rather stand outside the doors to watch and look and wait.

They'll never know the joys of life until it's passed them by,
And when they've reached the end of life, they'll regret they did not try.

There is a door we let God in; it lies within our hearts,
And if he comes inside this door he never will depart.

So when we enter life's last door the great and pearly gate,

It's there we will know the doors in life were sealed for us in fate.

The Forgotten Path
(For Dartha Roberts on her 70th birthday)

There once was a path not so long ago, which many people daily walked down. The path was worn, but well loved by many. It led through valleys to beautiful places, which brought peace to the heart of many.

One day people got tired of the old path and sought to find a new one, though no path was as beautiful as the old. The beauty of the path was still the same, but the people were tired of what it had to offer, so they broke in a new trail which didn't lead them to the brook where the spring continually ran or to the valley which led to the mountain side where peace flowed freely. They thought because this trail was new it would be more exciting.

The old trail grew high with grass, weeds, thistles, and thorns because no one ever took its route. What remained was still to be seen, felt, and loved. Though the path was hidden and covered up, it still was no less beautiful and still led to peaceful lands.

Just because we tire of something we should not forget its beauty and value nor give it up for something far less worthless. We've given up the old paths of our upbringing and traded it in for things pleasing to man and not God. Given up its holiness and its beauty for the paths of pleasure and self. When will man wake up and see how Satan has robbed him. Just maybe when it's too late.

LaVergne, TN USA
12 November 2010
204655LV00002B/2/P